ADRIANA LUNA CARLOS

Editor-In-Chief, Designer and
Co-Founder

HANNA OLIVAS

Managing Editor & Co-Founder

SUCCESS
SAVVY

**ADVERTISING
OPPORTUNITIES**

Info@SheRisesStudios.com

SHE RISES
S T U D I O S

CONTACT US

SheRisesStudios@gmail.com
www.SheRisesStudios.com

www.SheRisesStudios.com

FENIX INNOVATION *APRIL 2024*

LETTER FROM THE EDITORS

Dear Readers,

Welcome to the April 2024 issue of Success Savvy Magazine!

In this edition, we are thrilled to feature Cindy Witteman on our cover—a shining example of resilience, determination, and achievement. Cindy's article, centered on the transformative power of action, serves as a beacon of inspiration for all of us embarking on our own paths to success.

Success Savvy Magazine is more than just a publication; it's a testament to the limitless potential within each of us. Created for both men and women, our mission is to break barriers and redefine what it means to be successful. We cover all areas of success and savvy living, providing a platform to showcase high-achieving individuals like Cindy and share strategies for personal and professional growth.

Whether you're seeking career advancement tips, entrepreneurship insights, or ways to enhance your overall well-being, Success Savvy Magazine has you covered. Our pages are filled with expert advice, inspiring stories, and actionable steps to help you rise, elevate, and achieve success in every aspect of your life.

As we journey through the pages of this issue, let Cindy's story and the wisdom shared by our contributors ignite a fire within you—a fire of action, determination, and relentless pursuit of your dreams. Together, let us rise above limitations, elevate our potential, and achieve greatness.
Thank you for being a part of the Success Savvy Magazine. Here's to a month of growth, inspiration, and unstoppable success.

Warm regards,

Adriana Luna Carlos and Hanna Olivas
Editors of Success Savvy Magazine

FEARLESS ACTION:
CINDY WITTEMAN'S KEY TO SUCCESS

From the heart of Texas, Cindy Witteman radiates warmth and purpose, captivating those around her with her infectious energy and sincerity. As the driving force behind "Force" Magazine, Cindy wears many hats - she is a Business Owner, Speaker, Action Mastery Coach, Non-Profit Founder, and bestselling author. Her influence extends globally through her TV show "Little Give" and podcast "Is Manifesting Bullshit."

At the heart of Cindy's dedication is her role as an Action Mastery Coach, serving as a fundamental aspect of her passion. Through her extensive experience as a life and confidence coach, she discovered the pivotal role of action in achieving tangible results. Cindy observed that despite imparting impactful advice, her clients often struggled to make progress without taking decisive steps towards their goals.

Determined to bridge this gap, Cindy developed a tailored approach to assist her clients in taking constructive and sustainable action through incremental steps. She instilled in them the belief that there is no such thing as failure, only opportunities to learn and grow. With this empowering mindset, Cindy's clients gradually gained confidence in their ability to take action and make meaningful strides towards their aspirations. But why does action often seem daunting?

According to Cindy, it's rooted in the fear of the unknown, akin to the apprehension felt by a child whose parents turn off the lights in their room. Despite nothing changing in the room, the fear of uncertainty paralyzes the child from taking the simple action of turning the light back on. Cindy encourages others to confront this fear and metaphorically switches on the light in their minds, liberating themselves from the shackles of uncertainty.

Cindy underscores the importance of action in achieving success. She shares practical strategies for maintaining motivation that resonate deeply with her audience, empowering them to overcome obstacles and pursue their goals with unwavering determination. Cindy's insights on striking a balance between action and planning inspire a mindset of continuous growth and development. Her own personal journey serves as a testament to the power of perseverance, demonstrating how resilience and determination can lead to profound transformation.

With resolute conviction, Cindy shares her goals and aspirations, urging others to embrace their full potential and chart their own paths to success. Her story isn't just one of triumph - it's a narrative of resilience, empathy, and a belief in the transformative power of action. As Cindy continues to inspire and empower others, her legacy will forever be defined by her remarkable ability to effect positive change, one life at a time.

To gain a deeper into Cindy's remarkable journey, readers are invited to explore her upcoming book, "Beyond the Smile," set to release in May 2024. This candid memoir offers an insightful glimpse into Cindy's personal journey, chronicling her triumph over generational poverty, domestic violence, and single parenthood. Through "Beyond the Smile," Cindy aims to inspire individuals to recognize the innate power within themselves to shape their futures and embark on their own journeys of empowerment and self-discovery.

CONNECT WITH CINDY:

🌐 www.linktr.ee/cindy.witteman

📷 www.instagram.com/Cindy.Witteman

📘 www.facebook.com/profile.php?id=100089195777362&mibextid=LQQJ4d

The Secret to Building a Dreamy & Sustainable Business.

Written By: Lourdes Auquilla

Making $100,000 in sales is not the secret to building a dreamy business. One can make $100,000 in a year, but have $90,000 worth of expenses. This leaves them with $10,000 to take home (before taxes). How can they live their dream life with this income?

This is a simplified version of the numbers seen with business owners who show off their sales reports on Instagram. This ends up creating pressure on other entrepreneurs who are also growing their businesses.

Now, this is not trash talking coaches. Rather, the focus should shift away from making those $10k months, and the real emphasis should be on what one should actually be focusing on. So, what is the secret to building a dreamy and sustainable business that allows one to reach all of their dreams?
Being profitable.

Profit equals sales minus expenses. In other words, it's what's left in the business after all expenses are accounted for. Do they know what their profit is?
If not, no worries. It's pretty easy to calculate if their bookkeeping or recordkeeping is done.

If this isn't done, one should consider getting the DIY simple bookkeeping system, Dreamy Sheets, which will automatically calculate this as income and expenses are entered. Simply go to www.lourdesauquilla.com/dreamy to grab a copy! If bookkeeping is already done, one is already 90% on track to understanding their profit.

Let's revisit the example stated at the start. Would one rather make $100k in sales, have $90k worth of expenses, and take home $10k (before taxes)?

Or would one rather have made $70k in sales, have $20k worth of expenses, and take home $50k (before taxes)? The second option seems more favorable.

It's a significant achievement to say, "I made 100k in sales!". But an even greater accomplishment is to say "I made $70k in sales, and had a profit margin of 71%!". Everyone has their own definitions of what their dream business and life looks like. But one fact remains constant amongst all of our dreams.

The business has to be profitable to achieve them. If one is left with little to no money in the business each month, how can they afford that dream house, dream office, or dream vacation?
Sure, money can be borrowed. But why do this, when one has the power to assess and adjust where money is coming from and going to in the business? Business owners are intelligent. They have the knowledge and power to build a profitable and sustainable business.

The first step to achieve this is to understand what is happening with the numbers. As a Latina Bookkeeper, it is her job to let business owners know where their money is coming from, going to, how much they're profiting, or if they're at a loss. Business owners are way too busy to manage this, and they'll be even busier as they truly start to focus on profit. So let her take care of their bookkeeping!

No matter what the profit is, with her monthly reports, business owners will feel empowered to raise prices with confidence or adjust expenses so that profits can grow. Check her out at www.lourdesauquilla.com to start building a profitable & sustainable business that will help live the dream life!

www.lourdesauquilla.com • IG: lourdesbookss
LinkedIn: lourdes-auquilla-526696190 • FB: lourdesauquillabookkeeping

Women and Life

Article Written By: Yolonda Lee
www.yolondalee.com

What is life? Each individual may define life differently based on their childhood, adulthood, circumstances, experiences, or other factors they may have encountered in their life.

Is life getting up every day going to a job or perhaps operating your own business? Is life seeing to the wellbeing of yourself, loved ones, and others? Is life our success? Is life our economic status? What really is life? Have individuals experienced or are experiencing a job where they are not content; however, to maintain a decent lifestyle of daily living to provide for themselves and their families, they deal with things they really do not want to put up with. However, when thinking about receiving that paycheck each week or biweekly and the responsibilities they have, it seems to have them captive to situations to hang in there. How about this? Is life living from day-to-day hoping for dreams to come true not knowing really when it will happen?

Life is everyone's source of faith, food, and favor. The scriptures let us know that faith is the substance of things hoped for and the evidence of things not seen (Hebrews 11:1). Also, the scriptures state that the just shall live by faith (Romans 1:17). Faith, whether one is a believer or not, is a part of life. Faith is a source to know that there is hope. Regardless of circumstances or situations, faith will allow one to see further than their current status of living and realize that there are opportunities for betterment. Faith is what will allow one to get to the next level in life beyond what they currently are in. To spark the faith in one's life, read, meditate, and trust upon the following faith scriptures:

Romans 1:17 • Hebrews 11:1 • Hebrews 11:6

Realize that it does not take a mountain of faith to move forward in the things of life. If one has faith the size of a mustard seed, they have enough faith that can move whatever mountain(s) may be hindering, sidetracking, or distracting them from their betterment.

Life is you! You have faith to pursue the things you desire in life. Life is you loving yourself. Life is you having self-respect, character, and kindness. Life is you being there for your loved ones and showing up for others in whatever you do but not forgetting to make time for yourself. Life is the simple things in life that can have significant meaning. Life is food. Not just natural food but what one consumes that is anything they allow themselves to consume that impacts their wellbeing.

Do they consume foods of negative talk, gossip, rumors, or unkind words? Life is a favor. Will they trust God for the favor that was predestined for them? Favor that will allow them to walk in open doors and opportunities designed for them that no one else can do it like them? Favor that will show up in their life beyond their own capabilities. Life is living in faith, consuming foods for their natural and spiritual life for good, and favor destined for them.

Therefore, it is hoped that this article will have a touch of life-changing impact to one.

One is encouraged to never give up on life. ❤️

How One Wildfire Survivor Triumphed Through Tremendous Loss

by: Amanda O'Mara

Amanda and her husband experienced shock after losing their dream home and belongings to a wildfire that ripped through their community, killing two people. She states it's an odd feeling to have a roof over your head one day and the next day not have one.

What do you do after you literally lose everything? When you have nowhere to go or jackets to keep you warm, you naturally go into survival mode. Quickly the couple learned to accept help from others when it came to money, shelter, and clothing. They fully credit their friends and community for keeping them on their feet when all hope felt lost.

Sometimes, O'Mara remembers something she long loved and lost. "As long as we make it out alive, the rest is just stuff," she says. "But then when you go through it you realize, wow, some of those things were your dog's ashes or jewelry handed down from your grandmother after many generations." You simply can't replace those or put a price tag on that.

You keep things to remember the past. Items hold sentimental value. The home for them symbolized years of hard work and a place of solitude. It's part of who you are or your identity. "When you experience such a large loss, it's like a piece of you died in the fire too," she quotes.

Grieving a home full of memories and meaning is a process. And the loss didn't end there for O'Mara...

Since it was during Covid, building costs skyrocketed, leaving them hundreds of thousands of dollars underinsured. And O'Mara's business completely fell apart. Amanda ran a business helping online health and fitness professionals build an online business from the ground up. This type of work takes a lot of mental strength. "I was struggling coaching my clients when I was having daily panic attacks," she says. "How can I coach when I can barely take care of myself?" She paid the last of what she had in her bank account to her team member to finish coaching her current clients.

She was in survival mode for months to follow until she finally settled into a comfortable replacement home to begin rebuilding not just her home but her mindset as well.

"The first thing I bought after the fire was a journal from Target. I knew if I wanted to have the strength to keep going, I had to go inward first."

"Every single day I would start by listing as many things I was grateful for. When you do this you will learn how truly amazing and fortunate we are. It could be as simple as the toes on your feet or the stars in the sky...there is still SO much to be grateful for." She credits most of her comeback by a simple daily gratitude practice.

She also did EMDR therapy, plant medicine, and lots of energy healing work with spiritual leaders. Day by day, her strength came back both physically and mentally. She and her husband rebuilt their home themselves one nail at a time. She also re-launched her business which came back tenfold. She now has an incredible team who are all on a mission to help as many health and fitness professionals build their own business online to impact the masses by helping them with their health and fitness transformations.

O'Mara isn't stopping there either. She plans to build other similar businesses that will help others heal and grow using a variety of energy healing modalities.
She believes this work will create a ripple effect all around the world by helping others to let go of trauma, heal from chronic and mental illnesses, and grow by helping each person see their true potential and purpose in life.

"With intention and willingness, I truly believe the bandaid on the world can finally be ripped off so people can breathe a breath of fresh air and love and light can shine brighter with each and every individual," says Amanda.

🌐 www.amandaomara.com

in amanda-o-mara-7a573017

f amanda.omara

📷 amanda_omara

Nancy Rose

Her Story...

Nancy Rose's story is one of resilience, transformation, and unwavering determination. Divorced at a relatively young age with three children to care for, she found herself at a crossroads, grappling with the challenges of single parenthood while navigating her career in IT. Despite her professional success, a lingering sense of emptiness gnawed at her, driving her to seek something more meaningful in life.

It was during this period of introspection that Nancy stumbled upon "Celestine Prophecy," a book that would serve as a catalyst for her spiritual awakening. As she delved deeper into metaphysical concepts and explored alternative avenues of personal growth, she began to unlock a newfound passion for the esoteric world of metaphysics.

With each course she undertook and every book she devoured, Nancy felt herself drawn further into the realm of spirituality, gradually realizing that her true calling lay beyond the confines of her corporate career. Yet, as she straddled the divide between her burgeoning spiritual interests and her professional responsibilities, she faced a dilemma: how could she reconcile these seemingly disparate aspects of her life?

Inspiration struck in the unlikeliest of places: a viewing of "5th Element," a science fiction film that resonated deeply with Nancy's innermost desires for integration and synthesis. Drawing inspiration from the movie's themes of elemental balance and transcendence, she embarked on a journey of self-discovery and self-expression, culminating in the creation of Quintessence Creations.

Quintessence, the fifth and highest element in ancient philosophy, symbolized the essence of a thing in its purest form—a fitting metaphor for Nancy's mission to help women reconnect with their authentic selves. Through her business, she sought to bridge the gap between the material and spiritual realms, offering a sanctuary for soulful exploration and personal growth.

As Nancy's entrepreneurial journey evolved, so too did her approach to serving her clients. Recognizing the limitations of traditional brick-and-mortar establishments, she embraced the digital landscape, transitioning towards online courses and coaching programs to reach a wider audience. This pivot not only expanded her reach but also allowed her to adapt to the changing needs of her clientele in an increasingly digital world.

Yet, amidst the whirlwind of professional pursuits and personal growth, Nancy remained grounded by her steadfast commitment to family and community. Despite the transient nature of relationships in her life, she cherished each moment shared with those who walked alongside her, recognizing that parting ways often signaled a new chapter in their individual journeys.

For Nancy, the journey towards self-realization is an ongoing process—one marked by moments of clarity, epiphany, and divine timing. Through her own experiences of trial and triumph, she has come to understand the importance of perseverance, intuition, and faith in oneself. She encourages others not to give up on their dreams, even in the face of adversity, trusting that the universe has a plan far greater than we can imagine.

In essence, Nancy Rose's story is a testament to the power of resilience, transformation, and unwavering belief in the pursuit of one's passions. Through her work, her words, and her unwavering commitment to empowering women, she continues to inspire others to embrace their authenticity, pursue their dreams, and become unstoppable forces for positive change in the world.

www.EmbodyYourAuthenticSelf.com

UNLEASHING COURAGE WITH JOAHNA TUPAS
PATH TO PURPOSE AND PASSION

In her remarkable journey through life, Joahna Tupas embodies the very essence of grit, courage, purpose, and passion. Raised amidst the vibrant culture and warmth of the Philippines, Joahna's formative years were steeped in a love for learning and a deep appreciation for life. From an early age, Joahna displayed an innate curiosity and a hunger for knowledge, traits that would shape her path in profound ways.

In 2004, amidst the bustling energy of her college years, Joahna took her first bold step into the world of entrepreneurship. Fueled by a burning desire to revolutionize the freelancing landscape in her homeland, she launched her own Multimedia Arts Production Company. With a vision as vast as her ambition, Joahna sought to provide innovative opportunities for digital nomads to showcase their talents and connect with top-tier clients. Collaborating with a diverse array of artists and creatives, Joahna's company quickly gained recognition, attracting esteemed clients as a visionary entrepreneur.

However, Joahna's journey was far from linear. Driven by a deep-seated desire to make a meaningful impact in the realm of education, she made the bold decision to transition into academia. Drawing upon her wealth of industry expertise and entrepreneurial acumen, Joahna embarked on a new chapter as a college professor. In this role, she dedicated herself wholeheartedly to inspiring and empowering the next generation of leaders, instilling a sense of purpose and passion in her students, encouraging them to dream big and pursue their goals with unwavering determination.

As fate would have it, Joahna's journey took another unexpected turn when she found herself drawn to the field of Special Education. Embracing this new challenge with characteristic zeal, she transitioned into a role as a Special Education Teacher in Arizona, USA, where she currently resides. In this capacity, Joahna brings her unique blend of creativity, empathy, and determination to bear as she works tirelessly to support and uplift students with diverse needs. Beyond her professional endeavors, Joahna's personal interests and passions serve as a constant source of creativity and joy. An avid traveler, she finds solace and enrichment in exploring new cultures, immersing herself in diverse experiences, and embracing the beauty of the world around her.

An ardent music aficionado, Joahna finds harmony and rhythm in the melodies that accompany her on life's journey, adding a symphonic dimension to her diverse experiences. As a sports enthusiast, she thrives on the adrenaline rush of pushing her physical limits, embracing new challenges, and discovering the depths of her own capabilities.

In everything she does, Joahna is guided by a profound sense of purpose and a deep commitment to making a positive impact in the world. She attributes much of her success to the invaluable lessons she learned from her entrepreneurial mentor, her late father, Pastor and businessman Josefino Estrevillo. Additionally, she draws inspiration from her empowered muse, her mother, Carmelita Estrevillo, whose unwavering support and guidance have been a constant source of strength throughout her journey. At the core of Joahna's being is her unwavering faith in the Divine and her belief in the power of grace to guide her path. She breathes, lives, and moves through life with a deep sense of gratitude and humility, recognizing the abundant blessings that surround her each day.

As a speaker and author, Joahna is passionate about sharing stories of courage, resilience, and determination in the world. Through her words and her actions, she seeks to inspire and empower others to embrace their own journeys with courage, purpose, and passion, and to discover the extraordinary potential that lies within each and every one of us.

Partnered with her husband, Joahna is committed to ensuring the future of their son, embodying their shared values of empathy and dedication. Currently serving as the Founder and Chief Consultant of School in a Backpack since 2014, she aims to foster leaders instilled with confidence, compassion, and courage, guiding them toward fulfilling lives driven by their purpose. Her dedication to transforming education is evident in this initiative, empowering children to explore, learn, and evolve in ways that reshape their futures. Joahna's journey and pursuits stand as a well-spring of motivation, illustrating the limitless opportunities that emerge when we embrace our potential and pursue excellence.

Youtube: @joahnatupas • LinkedIn: joahnatupas
FB: joahnatupas • IG: joahnatupas

Colleen Brown-Chambers

Colleen Brown-Chambers, a seasoned leader and the driving force behind G.E.I.N Transformational Enterprise, is gearing up to launch her latest literary masterpiece, "She's Evolutionary". With a profound dedication to women's empowerment in the business realm, Colleen's creative fusion of poetry and personal development promises to be a groundbreaking contribution to the self-evolution journey of women worldwide.

Drawing on her rich tapestry of experiences and expertise in leadership, management, and personal development, Colleen has carved out a niche for herself as a trailblazer in the field of holistic success. Through her strategic workshop programs and transformational coaching presentations, she has empowered countless individuals to transcend perceived limitations and embrace their true potential.

Colleen's forthcoming book, "She's Evolutionary", is a testament to her unwavering commitment to fostering a culture of self-discovery and personal growth among women in business. Through poignant poetry and introspective prose, Colleen invites readers to delve into the depths of their being, unraveling layers of self-awareness and empowerment along the way.

By infusing her poetic narrative with themes of resilience, authenticity, and empowerment, Colleen offers a unique lens through which women can navigate the complexities of personal and professional growth. "She's Evolutionary" serves as a beacon of inspiration for women seeking to forge their path with courage, grace, and unwavering authenticity in a world that often demands conformity.

Beyond her literary pursuits, Colleen's impact extends far and wide. As a Justice of the Peace for St. Andrew and a passionate advocate for societal upliftment, she has orchestrated transformative initiatives such as the Men's Empowerment Workshop and the Legacy Tour for Boys, underscoring her commitment to fostering positive change at both individual and community levels.

In the realm of publishing, Colleen's vision knows no bounds. With her upcoming release, "She's Evolutionary", and the forthcoming "Lead-Your-Ship Workbook", tailored for small business owners and corporate leaders, she continues to push the boundaries of conventional wisdom, offering innovative strategies and tools for leadership excellence and personal development.

As Colleen Chambers shines a light on the transformative power of self-evolution through "She's Evolutionary", she invites women to embark on a journey of self-discovery, authenticity, and empowerment, illuminating the path to personal and professional fulfillment in the ever-evolving landscape of business and beyond. "She's Evolutionary" is now available on Amazon and Sangster's Book Store at Sovereign Center and Springs Plaza (Kingston, Jamaica).

🌐 **www.geintransformational.com**

📷 **@colleenchambersja**

📷 **@geintransformational**

Dr. Dominique M. Carson, LMP: Honoring a Trailblazer in Action or Sassy, Classy, Unstoppable & Dynamic: The Essence of Dr. Dominique M. Carson, LMP

Dr. Dominique M. Carson, LMP, is an award-winning freelance journalist, licensed massage practitioner, author, and orator. Carson's work has been featured in several publications, including Ebony.com, The Grio, NBC News, Singersroom.com, Bleu Magazine, Virginian Pilot, Preferred Health Magazine, Soultrain.com, Education Update, and Brooklyn news media outlets. She has interviewed over 100 notable figures in entertainment, such as Charlie Wilson, Regina Belle, Patti Labelle, Kirk Franklin, and many more. She also collaborated with Brooklyn historian and journalist Suzanne Spellen and launched a 118-page journal on Lefferts Manor, a neighborhood in Brooklyn. Carson also served as Program and Communications Coordinator for Man Up! Inc., a nonprofit organization in East New York, Brooklyn. While at the organization, she received a citation from the New York City Council and the "It's My Park Award" from the Partnership for Parks for community engagement in her hometown, East New York, Brooklyn. In November 2020, she released her first solo book, a biography on R&B icon Jon B titled "Jon B: Are You Still Down." Although published independently, "Jon B: Are You Still Down" was an Amazon Hot New Release in One Hour Biography and Memoirs Short Reads. It was also featured in Book Authority's 7 Best New R&B Music Books To Read, Goodreads, and Readers' Favorite in 2021. A year after the Covid-19 pandemic, she participated in the National Women's History Museum's journaling project titled "Women Writing History: A Coronavirus Journaling Project." In a 42-page journal, she shared how the COVID-19 pandemic impacted her life and career as a media analyst and massage provider.

Carson graduated from the City University of New York, Brooklyn College, with her bachelor's and master's degrees before age 25. She was also the first African American to receive the Brooklyn College Wall of Fame award in the winter of 2011. Her post-college life consists of writing articles and books and adding another venture, massage therapy. In 2019, she received her Associate of Applied Science degree and license in Massage Therapy from CUNY Queensborough Community College. She can practice massage with her credentials in her hometown, New York City, 44 other states, and Puerto Rico. She has received numerous awards, including 2x Author All-Star, the Global Iconic Changemaker Award, The Empowered Woman Award, and the Global Recognition Award for her editorial and health/wellness work. She was also awarded an Honorary Doctorate in Humanitarianism from the Global International Alliance Advocate University in Spring 2024. Her story has been featured in prestigious media outlets such as Sheen Magazine, Impact Magazine, Femi Magazine, Industry Times, and Forbes, as well as VoyageLA, ShoutoutLA, and Bold Journey.

Although the East New York Brooklyn native accomplished several milestones, she endured setbacks; she was hearing impaired as a child, experienced a severe asthma attack as a child that put her life at stake, was a survivor of child sexual abuse, lost one of her high school classmates to suicide, lost seven family members before she was 25, had to revive her career as a massage practitioner after her second career was shut down temporarily due to the pandemic, learned how to adjust in Virginia, the Old Dominion state during the pandemic in April 2020 after leaving her hometown, New York City, her comfort zone for 29 years, endured a near-fatal car accident in February 2023, and lost her teenage friend and sister to breast cancer in August 2023. But, through it all, she credits her Heavenly Father for His everlasting mercy, goodness, and grace over her life. The scriptures Matthew 19:26 and Jeremiah 29:11 motivate her to push through when life can sometimes be problematic. She also pays homage to close-knit family, friends, mentors, and colleagues for truly celebrating her deportment and journey. She understands that her accolades are prestigious and well-deserving; however, she wants her story to encourage everyone, especially East New York natives, that along with success comes responsibility, and you have to produce and aim to be efficient in and out of the workplace. Carson's mission is to facilitate people's lives with her hands and words.

Dr. Dominique M. Carson, LMP

LINKTR.EE/DOM0922

Brittney Golden

Golden Wealth Group (GWG) is driven by a deep-seated passion for entrepreneurship and financial empowerment, propelling them toward establishing generational wealth and fostering positive change. With a decade of experience, GWG has expanded to encompass various roles in financial services, real estate, tax preparation, customer service, and sales. Their primary mission is to assist families in navigating key life milestones, from college planning to retirement and addressing unexpected financial challenges. They offer life insurance solutions with living benefits, ensuring comprehensive financial security.

Beyond traditional financial services, GWG takes pride in guiding families to their dream homes as licensed Realtors.
Simultaneously, their involvement in revitalizing distressed properties contributes to community safety, enhances desirability, and boosts property values. The overarching goal at GWG is to empower individuals and families to achieve financial independence while positively impacting communities. This journey showcases the transformative power of passion, expertise, and unwavering dedication to creating lasting positive change.

Goldenweathgrouptx.com • IG: missbgolden

A Mother's Journey to Success in Solo Parenting and Entrepreneurship

by: Sana Naseer Sheikh

In the bustling city, amidst the chaos of life's challenges, one woman's story shines as a beacon of resilience and determination. Meet Sana Naseer Sheikh, a dedicated mother and a dynamic entrepreneur, whose journey is a testament to the power of perseverance and passion.

Sana's journey began with a dream to provide her son with a healthy environment, despite the challenges of solo parenting. Starting her career as a journalist, she quickly realized the importance of education in shaping young minds. With this insight, she transitioned into the education sector, where she dedicated 14 years of her life to serving her community.

However, life had other plans, and the arrival of the COVID-19 pandemic brought unprecedented challenges. Like many others, Sana found herself at a crossroads, her career in jeopardy and her son's well-being at stake. Undeterred, she took a leap of faith and founded Step Lab for Kids, a platform dedicated to providing educational resources for children.

Embracing the virtual world, Sana embarked on a new adventure, teaching students worldwide through online platforms. Despite the initial challenges, Sana found joy and fulfillment in connecting with students from diverse backgrounds, enriching their lives through education.

As her virtual teaching venture thrived, Sana's entrepreneurial spirit soared. She launched Emsm.lz, a brand that offers a wide range of handcrafted accessories and products. Each item is crafted with love and care, reflecting Sana's commitment to quality and creativity.

But Sana's journey didn't stop there. She expanded her horizons, venturing into broadcasting and digital marketing. Under her production company, Sana organized campaigns, events, and features that highlighted stories and perspectives from around the globe.

Through sheer determination and hard work, Sana transformed her challenges into stepping stones to success. Her story is a reminder that with passion and perseverance, anything is possible. Today, Sana is not just a mother and an entrepreneur; she is a source of inspiration for many, proving that with a strong will and a clear vision, one can overcome any obstacle and achieve greatness.

In conclusion, Sana's journey is a testament to the power of resilience and determination. From a solo parent facing economic hardships to a successful entrepreneur and educator, she has proven that with unwavering dedication, one can turn dreams into reality. Her story is a beacon of hope for anyone facing challenges, reminding us all that success is not defined by circumstances, but by the courage to pursue our dreams.

Tiktok: @sunzbuzz • IG: emsm.lz • FB: emsm.lz

SONYA WARREN

Sonya Styles is a growing hair braider/stylist from Inglewood, CA. Joining the beauty industry well over ten years ago was a dream she always had as a child; learning how to braid from her mother with the intention of being able to do her own hair after seeing her do it for so many years.

She is a licensed cosmetologist specializing in natural hair health and braids. There's a constant educational factor that she tries to instill in all of her clients to keep their hair healthy and growing at its best. She has learned plenty of what not to do vs what to do in this industry but the best thing as of recent is "Pray through the process and It's okay to take risks." And with guidance from her mentor Angelle SupaStar, she stays motivated and her family keeps her determined. This is just the beginning for her. -*S. Styles*

HairByStyles.as.me
IG: iam.styles • IG: _stylesapparel • Tiktok.com/iam.styless

Juwell Harley

Dr. Juwell Addis Harley hails from the beautiful Caribbean island of Jamaica. She is a proud mother of a humble lion whom she has named Jazz, and her hobbies include singing, playing the piano, cooking, mentoring, and philanthropy. She holds a Bachelor of Science Degree in Nursing, a Master's in Education, and a Doctor of Philosophy in Humanities.

The genesis of her book, Phun Phacts Pharmacology, came about when she became a lecturer of the course Pharmacology; she realized students were struggling to understand the concept, so she decided to simplify the content. The same has been tested and proven to be positively impactful.

Her cosmetic line came about as a result of her love for naturality and being a vegan/pescatarian all her life. She has realized that the masses embrace beauty products; however, many experience side and adverse effects. With Regal Hemprezz Cosmetics, everything is vegan, hypoallergenic, and brings out that authentic radiance.

She is also Co-Founder of a philanthropy organization known as tech-savvy-nurse, which merges technology with the nursing profession and provides necessities needed for research. In addition, they secure grants/scholarships for student nurses, supply equipment such as BP machines, thermometers, SAT machines, laptops/tablets for those in need, in order to make their journey through nursing school more manageable.

As Nelson Mandela stated, "education is the most powerful weapon in which you can use to change the world," she stands firm in honoring the same. As a change agent, she believes to have an impact on others; they should be approached with proof. Through education, she has learned that knowledge conquers all and has used her knowledge to nurture many in and out of the medical/professional sphere. Education has molded her into the phenomenal being she is, portraying good work ethics, meticulousness, and altruism while doing the same. Through education, she has met people whom she emulates; they have been her guide and inspire her to keep going.

Business-wise, it is her aim to nourish the minds of individuals pursuing their dreams in the nursing field and also beautify the bold with natural products. It is all about being beautiful with brains. She is also available to anyone around the world who is in need of mentorship or would like assistance through their studies.

REGALHEMPREZZ.COM
FB: JUWELL.HARLEY • IG: NURSEPIONEER

Shannon Salge

Shannon has always had a passion for health & fitness! But after being a manager at a gym for a few years, she realized that women weren't getting all the help she felt they deserved or needed in a traditional gym setting. She wanted to build a business that helped women not only with nutrition & training but also with functional lab testing, mindset work, and a different level of accountability. One of the initial challenges was people thinking that in-person coaching was the way to get them to their goals best. But after clients spend a few weeks in her program, they appreciate her holistic viewpoint to their health journey and how much quicker they see progress!

The first thing she did when she wanted to start her own company was hire a business mentor. She believes that if one truly wants to succeed, and succeed quickly, they should invest in themselves to learn from people who have done it before them. Secondly, she ensures that she is in a business that she truly has a passion for. It's easy to get burned out, but when one loves what she does day in and day out, she can't help but keep striving for success.

Showing up regularly and confidently on social media is key nowadays. She loves talking about her program and all the amazing client transformations they've had. But, more importantly, she has loved providing free education and value to the people who consume her content.

Shannon believes that encountering significant hurdles along the way is inevitable but helps one grow stronger as an entrepreneur. In her first year of business, she spent a lot of time trying to hire team members to help her grow. But, the first people she hired weren't going to be the ones that aligned with the future vision of her business! So, she thinks that firing her first two hires and spending a ton of time finding the right fits for those positions (and then hiring two more) was the hardest but best thing that has happened! Spending the time trying to find the right fits on the front end and taking the time to train them properly is time well spent that will pay back tenfold.

Her advice for other women aspiring to reach six-figure success in entrepreneurship and overcome gender-related obstacles is to be unapologetically themselves. She believes that entrepreneurship is already draining enough, so they shouldn't waste their time trying to be someone they are not. They should spend time honing in on their craft, become exceptionally good at what they do, and people can't help but be attracted to them no matter what.

FB: shannon.salge • IG: shannonsalgefitness • Fb.com/groups/1298733640503815

Andrena M Phillips

Her entrepreneurial journey has been a thrilling rollercoaster ride, filled with challenges and triumphs, but worth every moment. Leaving her legacy and making a positive impact on this world has been the most fulfilling aspect. What brings her immense joy is inspiring fellow women to embrace their true potential, play out loud, and shine brightly without fear. The inspiration to start her own business came during a difficult phase in her life. She felt isolated, broken, and lacked the support to love and believe in herself fully. Realizing the need to become her own source of strength and empowerment, she took charge of her life. She became the woman she was looking for.

Embarking on this entrepreneurial path was not without hurdles. Doubts and fears crept in, questioning her capabilities. However, she embraced failures as opportunities to learn and grow. Seeking guidance from mentors and immersing herself in industry knowledge helped overcome initial challenges.
Building a business from scratch requires persistence, resilience, and dedication. Embracing failure as a stepping stone to success was crucial. Today, her business stands as a platform to uplift and empower women, helping them find their strength and potential.

Scaling a business to six figures and beyond is a daunting challenge for many aspiring entrepreneurs. Her journey taught her several key strategies that were instrumental in achieving this level of success.
Setting clear and ambitious goals was paramount. She created a detailed roadmap with short-term and long-term targets, which kept her focused and motivated.
Adaptability and innovation were crucial to staying relevant in the fast-paced business world. She continuously improved products and services based on market trends and customer feedback.

Building a strong team of talented individuals who shared her vision was vital. Delegating effectively and trusting her team allowed her to concentrate on strategic decisions.

A customer-centric approach was also instrumental. Engaging with customers, valuing their feedback, and exceeding expectations created loyal advocates and increased word-of-mouth referrals. Investing in marketing and branding efforts expanded their reach and connected them with potential customers.

Lastly, she embraced continuous learning and self-improvement. Seeking advice from experienced entrepreneurs and staying updated on business strategies empowered her to make informed decisions.

By combining these strategies, she successfully scaled her business to six figures and beyond, creating a solid foundation for sustained growth and success. Aspiring entrepreneurs can use these tactics to navigate their own path to prosperity.

In today's digital age, building a strong brand and online presence is crucial. To attract high-paying clients or customers, she focused on developing and promoting her brand strategically. First, she defined her brand's unique value proposition and target audience. Then, she created a visually appealing and consistent brand identity across all platforms. Social media played a significant role; she engaged with her audience regularly, shared valuable content, and leveraged influencers to expand her reach. Additionally, she invested in search engine optimization (SEO) to improve online visibility. By prioritizing these efforts, she successfully attracted high-paying clients and customers to her business.

As an entrepreneur, facing setbacks is inevitable. A significant hurdle she encountered was being a single mother of three. Balancing business responsibilities and motherhood was challenging. To navigate through it, she prioritized time management, sought support from family and friends. She also hired reliable staff and delegated tasks. Embracing flexibility, staying focused on goals, and learning to ask for help were key to overcoming this obstacle and achieving success in both her business and personal life.

For women aspiring to reach six-figure success in entrepreneurship, her advice is to stay resilient and confident. She encourages them to embrace their uniqueness and leverage it as a strength. Seeking mentorship, building a supportive network, and never shying away from advocating for themselves are crucial steps. Believing in their abilities, being persistent, and not letting gender-related obstacles hinder their path to success is paramount.
In the pursuit of six-figure success, she advises women to remember this: Their journey as woman entrepreneurs may be filled with unique challenges, but within them lies a wellspring of strength, resilience, and unyielding determination.

She encourages them to embrace their power, rise above any obstacles, and let their light shine brilliantly. Believing in the incredible impact they can make, not just for themselves but for countless others they inspire along the way, is essential. Embracing their voice, their vision, and their worth, she emphasizes, will enable them to carve a path of greatness that leaves an indelible mark on the world. She urges them to go forth fearlessly, unapologetically empowered, and let nothing dim their flame, as the world is waiting for them to rise and lead the way!

keepmovinwithandrena.com • LinkedIn: AndrenaPhillips • IG: Keep_MovinWithAndrena

MEET JULIE RAMIREZ

Julie Ramirez is a busy mom of 3 who works alongside her husband helping families every day plan for the unexpected and build generational wealth through teaching basic financial literacy. She has a passion for helping families not go through what she endured after the loss of her mother and her father. Her business with her husband is unique as they have clients who don't have a clue where to start with their finances or who may be concerned they may not have the extra to save in their budget to those who are looking to help make their money work long term for them.

Julie Ramirez, a graduate from the University of South Florida, speaks of her husband Tony, "Tony and I have been married since 2003 and have been partners in life much earlier than that. Tony was my date for both homecoming and prom during my senior year of high school."

"We are both from Englewood, Florida, and after high school, Tony followed me to Tampa while I was attending USF, enrolled at Tampa Technical Institute and graduated in 2002 with a degree in electrical," says Ramirez. "We decided that Tampa would be our home and quickly planned to start a family." We had no idea that the happiest time in our life would turn tragic so suddenly.

In 2006, just a few short years after the Ramirezes were married, tragedy struck in Julie's family. "My Mom was diagnosed with a brain tumor in 2005, shortly after her 50th birthday, and we lost her in 2006," says Ramirez. It was unexpected and came suddenly after having my first child. I lost my mother at the most critical time you need your mom.

Again in 2011, more loss occurred. Both Tony and Julie lost their fathers, and Julie's younger brother, 15 at the time, needed a legal guardian. "I became a parent to my younger brother. My husband Tony stepped in and taught my brother how to drive and while it was difficult trying to fill that role, it was also difficult and challenging," says Ramirez.

"We soon realized that my Father had no will and I found myself maneuvering through the estate, which ended up in state probate court. The estate task was daunting at best and an eye-opener on the importance of being prepared for your loved ones if you pass." The life we had worked so hard to build was slowly crumbling down.

"Our partnership helps people in similar situations not go through what we experienced. Through this business, I have been able to connect with people who have relatable circumstances that I did. Helping with loss and picking up pieces," Ramirez says. "There must be a reason that I have this career. I can relate to these people and feel that God brings me to these people to help them through their circumstances."

Julie offers services to include - teaching financial literacy, game plans to reach financial goals, looking at investments for their long- and short-term needs, and constructing wills. From life insurance, retirement, college savings, investments, debt consolidation, and debt coaching, financial literacy coaching and refinancing. It's a total one-stop shop with personalized strategies to meet each family's financial goals. She works alongside her husband to help families every day plan for the unexpected as they crusade to help more families.

"All clients have become very close friends as opposed to simply business relationships," says Ramirez "Our business a way for us to regroup and put our energy into something positive from something so difficult." I understand what it's like to juggle grief and needing someone by your side to help you move through the tough decisions. That's what's key about me. If you are interested in connecting with her to see how she can assist you with your finances, you can reach her at tonyandjulieramirez.com.

www.tonyandjulieramirez.com

UNLOCK YOUR POTENTIAL: THE ULTIMATE SECRETS TO REACHING ATTAINABLE GOALS

WRITTEN BY: NICOLE ARSENEAU

Have you ever set a goal for yourself but struggled to achieve it? Whether it's a fitness goal, a career aspiration, or a personal milestone, we all have things we want to accomplish in life. However, the journey to attaining our goals can often feel overwhelming and even unattainable at times. But what if there were secrets to reaching those goals that could make the journey fun, rewarding, and achievable? In this article, we will explore the ultimate secrets to reaching attainable goals. So, if you're ready to unlock your potential and accomplish your dreams, let's dive in!

Focus on something, not everything: To make progress in your nutrition and training, focus on taking small steps forward in each area. Start by going to the gym, eating protein, or going for a walk. Identify your triggers: Recognize what causes you to self-sabotage. Is it stress, boredom, or a particular food? Once you identify your triggers, you can develop strategies to overcome them.

Schedule downtime for yourself: Practice gratitude and compassion for yourself. Avoid beating yourself up and make time in your calendar for self-care to help you recover and de-stress. Remember that change takes time and patience.

Measure it to manage it: Identify measures of progress that give you feedback about whether you need to adjust or pivot. Track your food, lift body measurements, hunger, stress level, or any other metric that is relevant to you.

Get support: Surround yourself with people who support your fitness journey. Join a like-minded group, find a training partner, or work with a coach if that's what you need to hold yourself accountable.

Use visualization and positive affirmations: Visualize yourself succeeding and achieving your goals. Use positive affirmations to reinforce your beliefs in your own capabilities and potential. This can help build resilience and emotional fitness.

Set realistic goals: Define specific, measurable, and achievable goals. Write them down and review them regularly to stay focused and motivated. Focus on progress, not perfection: Celebrate small wins and keep moving forward. Instead of striving for perfection, focus on making progress over time.

Be grateful for what you have: Practicing gratitude can help you maintain a positive mindset and stay motivated toward your health goals. Take time to appreciate the things you have, including your body and your health, and focus on the positive changes you're making to improve them.

Embrace Stoicism: Accept what is outside of your control, focus on what you can control, and practice emotional self-regulation. Build resilience through adversity: Setbacks, challenges, and failures are inevitable. See them as opportunities to learn, grow, and become more resilient. Use these experiences to practice resilience-building skills, such as adaptability, problem-solving, and positive self-talk.

Prioritize self-reflection: Take time to reflect on your thoughts, emotions, and behaviors, and assess how they are contributing to your overall health and well-being. This can help you identify areas for improvement and develop a deeper understanding of yourself.

In conclusion, reaching your goals is not just about sheer willpower and determination. It's about adopting a positive mindset, practicing self-reflection, and implementing effective strategies to overcome obstacles along the way. By focusing on progress, not perfection, and surrounding yourself with positivity and support, you can achieve your goals and live the life you've always dreamed of. So, remember to fuel your body and mind with proper nutrition and training, embrace new experiences, and be kind to yourself throughout the journey. With these tips and secrets, you can unlock your full potential and achieve anything you set your mind to.

Happy, Healthy, Successful: What 21st Century Women Know

by: Diana Elizabeth Martinovich

Hey girl, listen up. The rules have changed. Gone are the days when women were expected to choose between a career and family, play second fiddle to men, and sit around waiting to be rescued. You're in the driver's seat now. As a modern woman in the 21st century, you call the shots in your relationships, build the career of your dreams, and determine your own definition of success and happiness.

The women who are thriving today are the ones who know that real empowerment comes from within. They've learned that the secret to having it all is loving who you are, embracing self-care, and surrounding yourself with people who share your values and support your dreams. Stop waiting for someone else to make you happy or determine your worth. Happiness, health, and success on your terms - that's what being a 21st-century woman is all about. This one's for all you trailblazers out there rewriting the rules and blazing your own paths. The future is female, and the future is now.

What Does It Mean to Be a Successful Woman in the 21st Century?

What does it mean to be a successful woman in the 21st century? Success today looks different than in past generations. As women, we now have more choices and opportunities than ever before.

Education and Career

For many modern women, success means pursuing higher education and a career that inspires passion. Women today see that the sky's the limit - we can be scientists, CEOs, world leaders. Success is achieving your dreams and helping others along the way.

Financial Independence

Being financially independent and secure is important. Successful women take charge of their economic lives by earning their income, managing their money wisely, and planning for the future.

Relationships

Success also means surrounding yourself with people who love and support you. Strong, mutually caring relationships with partners, friends, and family are vital. Successful women value intimacy, honesty, and compromise in their relationships.

Health and Wellness

Taking good care of yourself is key. Exercising, eating right, limiting stress, and avoiding unhealthy habits help you feel your best so you can pursue your goals and enjoy life. Success means being active and energized, maintaining a positive outlook, and knowing when to unplug.

Contribution

Giving back to your community and society is a hallmark of success. Whether through volunteering, activism, or random acts of kindness, successful 21st-century women aim to make a positive difference in the lives of others in a way that's meaningful to them. In the end, being a successful 21st-century woman comes down to living according to your definition of success, following your passions, and making the choices that are right for you. Define your journey - and enjoy the adventure!

Achieving Work-Life Balance: How 21st Century Women Juggle Career and Family

Achieving work-life balance in today's world can be challenging, but modern women have found ways to make it work. Here are a few tips for juggling a thriving career and family:

Prioritize what's important

Decide what matters to you and focus on that. Don't feel pressure to do it all or be a "supermom." Learn to say no. Outsource when you can, like hiring a cleaning service or ordering takeout. Make time for self-care with exercise, hobbies, and socializing.

Set boundaries

Be clear in communicating your limits to employers and family. At work, discuss work hours and flexibility needs with your manager. At home, set technology-free times and be present when with family.

Share responsibilities

Don't shoulder the burden alone. Share chores and childcare with your partner as much as possible. Make schedules and divvy up tasks. Compromise when you disagree. Teamwork makes the dream work!

Take advantage of flexibility

If possible, look for jobs that allow telecommuting or flexible schedules. Make the most of maternity leave and paternity leave benefits. Use vacation and sick days when needed to attend school events or rest.

The keys to achieving work-life balance are making choices that align with your values, not being afraid to ask for what you need, sharing the load, and taking time for yourself. While it may require effort, the rewards of both a fulfilling career and a close-knit family are well worth it. Modern women can have it all - just maybe not all at once!

Self-Care Is Not Selfish: The Importance of Prioritizing Health and Happiness

Self-care is vital for 21st-century women who want to thrive. When you prioritize your health and happiness, you have more to give to others.

Make Time for Yourself

Carve out time each day just for you. Do something you enjoy, like reading a book, taking a bath, exercising, or calling a friend. Start with 15-30 minutes a day of dedicated "me time" and work your way up as needed. You deserve it!

Practice Self-Compassion

Be gentle with yourself. Learn to accept yourself as you are instead of harsh self-criticism. Speak to yourself with the same kindness and empathy you would show a close friend. You're doing the best you can, so avoid negative self-talk and forgive yourself for imperfections and mistakes.

Set Boundaries

Don't feel guilty about saying "no" to maintain your well-being. It's not selfish to establish limits and turn down requests that would overextend you. Make sure to also disconnect from technology like social media or emails during your time off.

Prioritize Good Health

Take good care of yourself by maintaining a healthy diet, exercising regularly, limiting unhealthy habits, and getting enough sleep every night. Your physical health impacts your mood and mental well-being. Stay on top of routine medical care and address any health issues to avoid future problems.

Pursue Your Passions

Engage in hobbies, creative pursuits, and activities that you find personally fulfilling and meaningful. Make the time to nurture your interests, talents, and dreams. Following your passions boosts happiness and life satisfaction. When 21st-century women practice self-care, they gain resilience, wisdom, and inner strength. By putting your needs first, you become empowered to face life's challenges with grace and poise while inspiring others. Make self-care a priority and choose happiness - you deserve nothing less.

Smashing Stereotypes: Overcoming Gender Bias in Male-Dominated Fields

As a woman in a male-dominated field, overcoming gender bias and stereotypes is an ongoing challenge. But the good news is, times are changing. With determination and perseverance, you can smash through stereotypes and glass ceilings.

Do Your Homework

Educate yourself on the scope of the role and the industry you want to enter. Be extremely well-versed in the skills, knowledge, and experience needed to excel in that position. Come prepared to every interview with specific examples of your relevant accomplishments and expertise.

Build Your Confidence

Don't doubt yourself or your abilities. Know that you absolutely have what it takes to succeed in this role. Speak confidently about your value and don't apologize for your ambition. Your confidence and competence will be evident to employers and colleagues.

Find Mentors and Allies

Seek out other women who have broken barriers in your industry. Build a network of mentors and allies who can guide you, support you, and help you navigate challenges. Their experience and encouragement can help boost your confidence and open new doors.

Speak Up and Take Risks

Make your voice heard in meetings and don't be afraid to share your perspectives and ideas. Take on high-visibility projects and stretch assignments to showcase your talents. Step up for leadership and advancement opportunities, even if you don't feel 100% ready. Have the courage to take risks - your male counterparts do.

Stay Resilient

Dealing with stereotypes and discrimination is frustrating and demoralizing. But don't get discouraged or deterred from your goals. Stay focused on your abilities and potential, not your gender. Remind yourself why you chose this path. With resilience and determination, you can accomplish amazing things.

The 21st-century woman is breaking barriers and clearing the way for future generations. With hard work and perseverance, you too can overcome obstacles, shatter stereotypes, and achieve your dreams. Success is within your reach. Now go get it!

Leaning in and Leaning on Each Other: The Power of Female Mentorship and Community
As women, we are stronger together. Forming mentorship and communities with other women is one of the most powerful ways we can support each other in living happy, healthy, successful lives.

Find Your Tribe

Seek out women with similar interests and life experiences. Join local women's networking groups, online forums, or start your meetup. Having a tribe of women who "get you" can help combat feelings of self-doubt and isolation. They can also introduce you to new opportunities and share advice for overcoming shared challenges.

Look for Role Models

Identify women who inspire you and have achieved what you aspire to. Don't be afraid to reach out to them. Many successful women are passionate about mentoring other women. Ask them out for coffee to learn from their experiences. Having role models shows you what is possible and helps you set meaningful goals.

Pay it Forward

Once you've found your footing, look for opportunities to mentor other women. Helping them along their journey is a way to give back to your community and continue the cycle of support. Your mentee may even become a close friend or future collaborator.

Lift Each Other Up

Rather than seeing other women as competitors, choose to support and celebrate each other. Promote their accomplishments, introduce them to key contacts, and help make new connections. When we work to lift each other up, we rise together.

Forming bonds with other women is vital to overcoming systemic disadvantages and biases that still impact women in the workplace and society. Together, we are stronger, wiser, and able to achieve great things. Make sisterhood and mentorship a priority - your happiness, health, and success depend on it.

Conclusion

So, there you have it, ladies. To be happy, healthy, and successful in the 21st century, focus on what really matters to you. Don't get bogged down comparing yourself to unrealistic societal standards or chasing some elusive notion of "having it all." Define what having it all means for you, and go after that. Surround yourself with people who love and support you. Take good care of yourself by maintaining a balanced diet, exercising, and managing stress. And follow your passions - whether that's advancing your career, volunteering, creative pursuits, or quality time with loved ones. The possibilities are endless for 21st-century women, so choose your path wisely and make the very most of this exciting time. The future is female, and the future is yours.

Now go get it!

CONNECT WITH DIANA

www.dianaemartinwrites.com
www.amazon.com/author/diana.elizabeth

www.facebook.com/dianaelizabethmartinovichauthor
www.instagram.com/dianaelizabethmartinovich

MOVING THROUGH EMOTIONAL BARRIERS:
UNDERSTANDING AND OVERCOMING EMOTIONAL RESISTANCE

Have you ever paid attention to that feeling that comes up any time you're doing something new in your business or your life? It could be emotional resistance.

Emotional resistance refers to the subconscious or conscious defense mechanisms that we use to protect ourselves from experiencing difficult emotions or situations. Emotional resistance can manifest in a variety of ways, such as denying or avoiding feelings, pushing away people or situations that trigger uncomfortable emotions, or distracting oneself from feelings through various coping mechanisms.

When we think about it logically, we can see that it is an inevitable part of the human experience, and we can expect to encounter it across our lifetime. Sometimes we are so used to the resistance being part of our reactions that they become automatic – a little like being on autopilot.

So, what might emotional resistance look like for you? It can manifest in a variety of ways, but for a lot of women, it might show up as…

- Getting distracted or letting other things become "bigger priorities" without any real reasoning.
- Overcomplicating what we 'have to do' as a way to slow yourself down and therefore 'put off' success or failure.
- Asking your friends and family what they think you should do rather than trusting yourself and your own intuition.
- Thinking that you know it all or feeling like you've tried it all and so there's no point trying again.
- Not setting aside the time to do 'the work' you need to, to move towards your goals.
- Quitting at the first sign of trouble or when the results aren't instant because "if it hasn't worked by now, it probably won't."
- Comparing yourself to others and feeling despair because you 'should' have done more with your life by now!
- Judging yourself for how difficult things are and then going into cycles of shame, blame, and guilt that prevent you from doing what you really want to do.
- Not doing anything until everything is perfect.

We can find that our emotional resistance is a response to loss, trauma, or past difficult life experiences. Our brain uses resistance to keep us safe by helping us to regulate our emotions and to manage the intensity of our feelings.

While this can protect us from making decisions that could be harmful, it can also stop us from stepping into spaces that help us develop and grow as humans. You'll know when resistance makes an appearance because ultimately you end up not doing the things you really want and need to do in order to create the results you aspire to.

It's important to be aware of emotional resistance and make sure you are checking and challenging where it is coming from and what it is trying to do. Using these simple but effective strategies can help you overcome resistance and ease the impacts it may be having.

- **Acknowledge and Find the Source of Your Feelings.** A useful first step is to recognize and name the emotions you are experiencing. Allow yourself to feel them without judgment or criticism. This may be difficult, but it is essential for moving forward. Ask yourself: What am I feeling? Why am I feeling this way? What is causing me to be resistant?

- **Talk It Out.** Talking out your feelings can often be helpful. Talk to someone you trust and feel comfortable with, such as a friend or family member, a coach, or therapist. Using others as a sounding board can help you gain insights and develop strategies to move past your resistance.

- **Practice Self-Compassion.** Self-compassion is simply treating yourself with kindness, understanding, and acceptance during times of difficulty or failure. It's about knowing that you are human, and you will feel fear and resistance and then responding by nurturing and supporting yourself.

Remember, although doing 'the work' can feel tiresome or even overwhelming, it's only once we have a better understanding of our feelings and have identified the source of our emotional resistance that we can begin to explore healthier ways of moving through the effects and achieving our version of success.

CONNECT WITH DIONNE
HTTPS://LINKTR.EE/COLLECTIVEWISDOMCOACHING

WRITTEN BY
MELANIE GREENHALGH

WEBSITE
WWW.COLLECTIVEWISDOMCOACHING.COM

Why Women Play It Small and How We Can Facilitate Change (Empowering women)

There's the age-old comparison between women and men and expectations of their roles in society, within the family, and at work. Many women, even today, undersell and undervalue themselves simply because it's ingrained in them since childhood through intergenerational beliefs and role biases.

Here's my take on the five reasons women tend to play it small:

Societal expectations

Women are 'expected' to play a certain role in society, and irrespective of the changes we make and see in the modern world, the outdated and typical archetypes of a patriarchal society still haunt us. Women are expected to fulfill the role of a domestic goddess, have a career, manage and nurture the family, be the strength behind her successful partner, and in doing all of those things and playing all of these roles, society still doesn't want her to play big, to own her power, to prioritize her Self and her needs because she should sit quietly in the background.

Fear of being vulnerable – Having been sold a dream and being let down numerous times, women build up walls to protect themselves from others not showing up for them the way they want and appreciate. To open up to others; the world and to let people see her real essence takes someone she can trust and her truth take her to discovering her power and being unafraid of knowing that she will learn lessons and course correct along the way. And not because she needs a knight in shining armor to rescue her when she opens up about her fears and as she develops her self-belief, but so she can express her concerns free from judgment.

Unsure of themselves – We have to ask ourselves whether we're building women up or if we're bringing them down, causing further damage? Many women are raised with conditions and structures where they subconsciously learn that they're not good enough or are reminded of their past experiences as failures. This leads to self-doubt in their present and future and keeps them limited and living a life where they fail to show up in their divine essence: powerful, beautiful, aligned with their Soul.

Fear of saying/doing the wrong thing

We think we have to get it right the first time round, so that our family, friends, and society view us in a particular way (through their conditioned views of what success looks like). We play it small because we fail to accept ourselves as beings who are constantly learning and growing and we struggle to offer ourselves and other women compassion as we move through our journey. Sometimes, we'll say or do things that may not necessarily go as planned and we have to accept that we will learn from these experiences.

Fear of being judged – Society is fast to place judgments on people in general, but often women do this to other women. When she's living in a world where both the men and the women are judging her decisions, movements, and dreams-what hope does she have? It's no wonder she's playing it small with all that support we're giving her! It's why she stays quiet, why she struggles to open up and be vulnerable. It's all related.

If we're not getting support from our friends and family, let's take responsibility for consciously creating a better environment for each other, as women for women. I say this because these are the things I've had to acknowledge and release to come into my true feminine power.

Here's what we can do to help women play big:

- Stay open-minded, or develop an open mind and be a supporter of women
- Be there for women and let them know it's safe, instead of criticizing or shooting their dreams down
- Build her up and affirm her and her intentions to play bigger
- Assure her that life is about learning and to take what she may be programmed to see as a failure as a learning lesson instead
- Consciously create safe spaces for other women, free from judgment and boost each other to show you're on her side.

If we all offer a little bit of support for each other, soon we'll begin to believe, and instead of letting setbacks stop us, we'll keep moving to achieve our goals and dreams. Let's remind each other and ourselves that it's okay not to get it right the first time. It's about showing up and focusing on creating the life we want for ourselves. Subscribe for free access to my Unblock your Self masterclass www.divya-chandegra.com/subscribe

 Unblock Your Self Masterclass   **Success Starts with Self**

3 Memorable Systems Everyone Must Know When You Find Your Self Blocked In Unhealthy Repetitive Cycles

Sign up for FREE so you can learn to...
- Respond instead of react
- Understand & develop a connection with your Self
- Create a better life for your Self
- Identify your behaviours & causes
- Start implementing the three systems today!

Were You Raised In An Over-giving Environment And Programmed To Always Put The Needs Of *Others* Before Your Own?

This eBook will set you up for long-term success in life, love and your career

All in one pdf:
Part 1: Wellness & Self-care
Part 2: Connections & Relationships
Part 3: Success & Growth

PHENOMENAL SUCCESS WITH SMARTER EMOTIONS: CONQUER DECISION-MAKING AND INCREASE YOUR EQ & REVENUE AS A FEMALE SOLOPRENEUR

ANNAMARIA BEREK

As a female solopreneur, you have the power to create financial freedom and build a successful business. However, the road to success can be filled with challenges such as making tough decisions and managing your emotions. You have to deal with so many other things in your life, taking on a business on top of it will test your endurance. But not to worry, it's a skill you can learn and implement! By learning how to make smarter & faster decisions, you can achieve phenomenal success and increase your revenue. You'll also master emotional intelligence (EQ) that'll give you an unfair advantage over other business owners!

To start, it's important to shift your mindset from that of an employee to that of a boss. As a boss, you have control over your business and your decisions. This mindset shift can help you overcome internal blocks that are stopping you from running a successful business.

Next, you need to conquer the challenges that come with decision-making as a solopreneur. By developing your EQ, you can increase your confidence, resilience, and leadership skills.

One method from With Annamaria that can help you make confident decisions is The 3-20-60 Decision-Making Method! How does it work? Choose three things you can't decide on whether it's a problem, a training, a platform, etc. Set the timer for 20 minutes for deciding which one to pick (spoiler: you can't go wrong with your decision but it's a whole other topic!) listing the pros and cons. Set the timer for 60 minutes creating the best course of action steps to make that one thing happen. By giving yourself a set amount of time to make a decision, you can avoid analysis paralysis and move forward with your plans.

By making decisions faster and with more confidence, you can increase your revenue. How? Your confidence will attract your ideal clients, you'll create time for building relationships, make sales, and allow you to stand out, take advantage of opportunities and stay ahead of the competition. Letting things go that don't serve you is an important decision as a business owner.

How else can you support your decision-making? You need to ensure you have the energy and focus needed to build a successful business. By taking breaks, practicing self-care, and seeking support when needed, you can improve your overall well-being and increase your ability to handle stress.

In conclusion, as a female solopreneur, it's important to keep up with the fast pace environment by being on top of your game not only with your marketing plan but with your Mindgame. By shifting your mindset, developing your EQ, and making decisions faster, you can achieve phenomenal success and create the financial freedom you desire.

xoxo
Annamaria

Mental Health In The Workplace

Written By: Laura Samson

Mental health in the workplace is an increasingly important topic in our modern society. According to a survey conducted by the International Labour Organization, more than half of the world's labor force is facing high levels of work stress, and nearly a third of workers suffer from burnout. Work stress disorders are the leading cause of absenteeism in many countries, and they have a considerable impact on the quality of life of workers.

We all face challenges and pressures that can affect our mental and physical well-being at work, but also in our relationships or in our daily lives. This is something I personally experienced after working for months in a grueling job: delivery driver.

What happened to me?

I worked for 55 to 60 hours a week in a job that did not allow me to express my creativity, whereas I am a photographer and graphic designer. Instead, I had to follow a monotonous routine, make deliveries and drive for long hours every day. I ran out of time and began to feel exhausted and disconnected from my passions and relationships.

I began to feel the effects of this exhaustion on my mental health. Two days in a row, I had panic attacks driving - thinking I was going to pass out and have an accident - which eventually led to burnout. I realized at the time that it was crucial to take care of myself and give up this position that heavily affected me. My body said stop. From then on, I started spending time with my friends again, cultivating my creative passions, and taking care of my physical health. By taking this 2 months break, I found my balance and was able to reconnect with the things that make me happy.

Taking breaks is really critical to our mental health and overall well-being. If you also have mental health issues, it is important not to judge yourself and feel guilty. Keep in mind that many people are going through difficult work-related times. Mental health is an essential part of our overall well-being and it is important to take it seriously.

Addressing the global crisis of mental health in the workplace: Strategies for employers.

Addressing workplace mental health issues requires both individual and collective action. Here are some tips on how to do this:

- Fostering a healthy work environment: Employers can implement mental health policies, provide training and establish employee support programs.
- Encourage breaks: It is important to encourage breaks and rest times for employees. Regular breaks help reduce stress and improve productivity.
- Promoting work-life balance: Employers can offer flexible work schedules, days off, or the ability to work remotely to help employees find that balance.
- Mental Health Awareness: Employers can organize mental health awareness events and provide training to help employees better understand and learn about mental health issues.
- Encourage communication: Employers should encourage open and honest communication between employees and superiors. This can help identify mental health issues and treat them quickly.

Instagram: https://www.instagram.com/smsn.studio/
Behance: https://www.behance.net/lauras20
LinkedIN: https://www.linkedin.com/in/laurasmsn/

Know that they are also many resources and options available to help you, including therapies, support groups, and stress management techniques such as meditation and yoga. It's also important to focus on your passions outside of work.

5 ways to take care of your mental health:

Taking care of your mental health is an important part of maintaining a happy and healthy life. Here are five things you can do on your own to improve your mental well-being:

- Practice mindfulness: Taking time each day to sit quietly and focus on your breath can help reduce stress and anxiety. Mindfulness can also help you feel more present and grounded in your daily life.
- Get moving: Exercise is a great way to boost your mood and reduce symptoms of depression and anxiety. Even just 30 minutes of exercise each day can make a big difference in how you feel.
- Connect with others: Maintaining social connections is an important part of overall well-being. Make time to connect with friends, family, and colleagues, even if it's just for a quick chat.

- Take breaks: It's important to take breaks throughout the day to give your brain a rest. Whether it's taking a short walk or just stepping away from your desk for a few minutes, breaks can help improve productivity and reduce stress.
- Practice self-care: Self-care means taking time to do things that make you feel good. This can be as simple as taking a relaxing bath or treating yourself to your favorite meal. Prioritizing self-care can help reduce stress and improve overall well-being.

Remember, taking care of your mental health is a process and it's important to be patient with yourself. By incorporating these simple practices into your daily routine, you can start to feel more centered, calm, and happy.

These actions are mandatory to maintain good mental health and help you feel happier and more balanced in your life. By taking care of yourself, you can regain your balance and live a happy and fulfilling life.

Faith over Fear

Tamara Shields

She grew up in a small town, and her childhood was just as challenging as any other child who grew up in the projects. However, she still managed to graduate from college and raise four boys. If there's anything that she's learned from having many trials and tribulations in her life, it's that you're always going to receive more Noes than Yeses, and you're also going to give out more noes. It's simply because our parents instilled no in us as children and society has instilled no in us as adults.

Therefore, the thought of operating outside the norm of what everyone else is doing can be terrifying. Sometimes we say no with no valid reason other than exercising our right to say no or we're afraid of what the results of yes look like. Although there is a place for no if saying yes leads you to a path of self-destruction, hurt, harm, or danger. However, the majority of the time we say or hear no is not from fearing we're in danger, but more so from a place of feeling that we won't succeed. In this case, no is considered to be the fear of failure. The truth of the matter is that we are creatures of habit and anything that challenges that, our natural instinct is to push back. Even if what we're currently doing hasn't worked or is no longer working, we are more likely to continue to do the same thing while expecting different results. The last time she checked, that was considered the definition of insanity. She believes it's fair to say that we've all had our share of insanity according to this. She too was guilty of binding this fear around her neck and restricting her right to say yes to her hopes and dreams. However, there came a point in her life when she decided that she would no longer be a victim to the word no. She began to view it as she just needed to keep going forward until she gets to the yes that she's looking for.

Instead of operating in fear, she chose to start operating in faith. The more she operated in faith, she soon found out that faith is like a muscle, the more you use it, the stronger it gets. Because of her faith, she has seen God move mountains in her life. Though she still receives many noes, her faith propels her towards the yes that God has for her. The results of the yes are so amazing, sometimes she forgets that no exists. If you really want to know how to get to this place of faith and align yourself with God's yes, children are our best teachers. They will ask you the same question over and over again until they get the answer they're looking for or if they receive a no from one parent, they just go ask the other, and if that's a no, they go to the grandparents which most likely ends with a yes. Although no has been instilled in them, they're still willing to explore the opportunity of receiving a yes. At times we too should be like children and explore the possibilities of what yes could be. So don't let the fear of receiving a no or the fear or failure stop you from following your hopes and dreams. Have faith that everything is working for your good, and just know that faith doesn't start off as big as a tree, it begins as a mustard seed, and it will grow over time.

www.facebook.com/tamarashields2020 | www.instagram.com/greenacresbrokerage | www.medicareenroll.com

Why Boss Bitch Vibes Leads To Burnout

First of all, you might be questioning what 'Boss Bitch Vibes' actually means?

In the Coaching Industry, we hear statements such as 'Boss Bitch Vibes' which encourage women to exert their authority by stepping into their masculine energy and leaving their natural feminine ow behind.

The Urban Dictionary denes Boss Bitch Vibes as 'A confident, successful and independent woman who speaks her mind and stands up for what she believes in. She keeps it 100% real with everyone, sets boundaries, and isn't afraid to go after what she wants.'

Whilst going after what you want can be perceived as 'courageous', it can also be very damaging to our health. In order to hit your goals, it requires you to step into your 'doing' energy, and too much 'doing' can cause an imbalance in energies. This imbalance can lead to burnout. The feminine energy has been associated with being 'weak' and more and more women have become disconnected from their natural state of ow by operating in their 'hyper-masculine energy' and 'doing' too much, not giving themselves time to rest.

The new paradigm.....
For years we have seen the coaching industry operate in a masculine matrix that has kept us trapped in a non-emotional state and causing a disconnect. The masculine energy is perceived by society as strong, and for ambitious women to be approved 'as good as a man' it has been encouraged to step into their 'boss bitch vibes'.
Things are changing! Our entire planet is moving into a natural feminine ow and we are moving away from these masculine traits that have kept many women suffocated and disconnected. Women are starting to 'awaken' and understand that to advance their careers, they cannot hide their true identity or suppress their underlying emotions.

The Masculine Vs Feminine paradigm
Masculine energy is the 'doing energy' which we use to get results. However, over the years, it has been encouraged so much within the workplace that we 'have' to do more in order to get more. This has led to a society of people disconnected from their feminine energy, by operating in our 'hyper masculine'.

Hypermasculine is when you operate too much in your masculine, this looks like feeling overworked, overanalyzing, being too logical & pragmatic, feeling burnt-out, constantly overthinking, unable to switch o, overdoing, and becoming obsessed and consumed with their day-to-day careers. All of these behaviors are driven from the belief that you have to 'do more to get more'.

But like everything, (just like Ying & Yang), we need both energies.
Contrary to the masculine energy, feminine energy is about ow. It is less about rational and logical-minded energy. It is more about using your internal guidance and intuition, that comes from the heart. It requires you to connect inwardly and hear the whispers of your own mind.

Mastering Your Energies
To achieve balance and consistently get success, we must master the duality of masculine and feminine energies.
As an Energy Expert, I help Women in business realign their energies by eliminating their emotional wounds which are driving their hypermasculine behaviours (overdoing & overworking).

How To Re-align Your Energy?

If you are a Woman in Business addicted to the 'hustle' and 'grind' then follow these my practical tips, to realign your energy and find your natural flow.

1. Find Your Inner Connection- whether that be meditation for just 5 minutes a day, going for a walk and connecting to nature, or breathe work. Find time each day to connect inwards. This gets you out of your logical brain (masculine energy) and centered into your heart (feminine energy).

2. Be Present - If you are always overthinking and thinking ahead, then you will nd it hard to be grateful for the now. Make 10 minutes a day to say 'thank you' for everything around you. This can simply be, day to days things such as feeling grateful for your warm cosy bed, your fridge full of food, or for your loving family. Take time to appreciate what you have around you and it'll bring you into the present moment.

3. Find a routine at bedtime that calms your mind - it is hard to sleep with a busy brain. The best techniques to slow your brain waves is to listen to a hypnosis or theta subliminals.

Try these top 3 tips and your energy will start to feel more in alignment and ow!

www.facebook.com/lornajaynelifestylebalance | www.Instagram.com/lorna_jayne_

Empowering Emotional Resilience: Practical Techniques for Better Results in Life

BY CHRISTINA ALDAN

It's time to get real about emotions in the workplace. We've all had those days where emotions run high, making it hard to focus on work. Whether it's a personal issue, conflict with a coworker, or feeling overwhelmed, we're still expected to manage our responsibilities in a professional manner. But how can we accomplish that? By hiding in the bathroom stall to silent-cry? That's a useful technique sometimes, but not as a daily strategy. Or by making more workplace rules? That seems to demoralize the company when the rules aren't fairly enforced. Unfortunately, neither of these solutions --hiding nor policing-- can stop emotions from arising in the workplace. The truth is that we can't simply policy emotions out of the workplace. However, we can teach communication skills by empowering people with tools for emotional resilience.

Here are three proven solutions I use to help my clients and mentees get better results in their personal and in their work lives:

1. Mental Health First Aid: Mental health issues are more common than you might think. According to the World Health Organization, one in four people in the world will be affected by mental or neurological disorders at some point in their lives. And they take those issues with them to work, to the grocery,

to the mall...wherever they go. This includes conditions such as grief, depression, and anxiety. So, it's likely that someone in your workplace is dealing with a mental health issue right now. Mental Health First Aid is a training certification program that teaches people how to recognize the early signs of a mental health crisis and how to provide support to someone who is experiencing one. By learning these skills, team members can use nuanced phrases to improve communication with someone who may be exhibiting early warning signs of a mental health crisis. Mental Health First Aiders also learn how to help someone in the midst of a crisis. This, in turn, reduces stress in the workplace. Research has shown that mental health first aid

can improve mental health literacy, reduce stigma, and increase confidence in providing support to others (Jorm et al., 2010). Having staff members who are trained to recognize and respond to a person who is struggling demonstrates a supportive workplace culture that values mental health.

Research supports the effectiveness of Mental Health First Aid (MHFA). A study published in the Journal of the American Medical Association found that individuals who received MHFA training had improved knowledge of mental health issues and were more likely to seek help for themselves or others. If you or someone you know would like to be certified in MHFA for Youth or Adults, please contact The Avery Burton Foundation (https://AveryBurtonFoundation.org) to find out how to join an upcoming cohort of learners.

2. Conflict Resolution: Conflict in the workplace is inevitable, but how we handle it can make all the difference. Learning conflict-resolution skills can help you resolve disputes with coworkers in a productive and respectful manner. Conflict resolution involves active listening, empathy, and finding a mutually beneficial solution. By using these skills, you can prevent conflicts from escalating and improve working relationships.

A study published in the International Journal of Conflict Management found that employees who received conflict resolution training had better job satisfaction, lower stress levels, and improved working relationships. So conflict resolution training can improve workplace outcomes. To help people practice these skills in a safe environment with strangers so you don't have to worry about retaliation (because who wants to practice dealing with tough emotions with your boss? Maybe

Money Talks: The Importance of Financial Literacy and How It Can Improve Your Life

Financial literacy is the ability to understand and effectively manage one's financial affairs. In today's world, financial literacy is more important than ever before. From credit card debt to retirement planning, the financial decisions we make can have a significant impact on our lives. In this article, we will explore the importance of financial literacy, the benefits of being financially literate, and some practical tips for improving your financial literacy.

Importance of Financial Literacy

Financial literacy is important for several reasons. Firstly, it enables individuals to make informed financial decisions. With a good understanding of financial concepts, individuals can make informed decisions about their investments, budgeting, and spending. They can also avoid financial scams and make better financial choices.

Secondly, financial literacy helps individuals to build wealth. By understanding financial concepts, individuals can take steps to increase their income, save money, and invest wisely. This can help them to achieve their financial goals and build a secure financial future.

Finally, financial literacy is important for the overall health of the economy. When individuals are financially literate, they are more likely to make responsible financial decisions that benefit both themselves and the wider economy.

Benefits of Financial Literacy

The benefits of financial literacy are numerous. Firstly, financially literate individuals are better able to manage their finances. They are more likely to have a budget, save money, and invest wisely. This can help them to achieve their financial goals and build a secure financial future.

Secondly, financially literate individuals are better able to avoid financial scams. With a good understanding of financial concepts, individuals can spot financial scams and avoid being taken advantage of.

Finally, financially literate individuals are more likely to be financially independent. By understanding financial concepts, individuals can take control of their finances and make informed financial decisions. This can help them to build wealth and achieve their financial goals.

Tips for Improving Financial Literacy

Improving your financial literacy doesn't have to be difficult. Here are some practical tips for improving your financial literacy:

1. **Read financial books and articles** - There are many books and articles available on financial topics. Read them to gain a better understanding of financial concepts.
2. **Take a financial literacy course** - Many community colleges and universities offer financial literacy courses. Consider taking one to improve your financial knowledge.
3. **Seek advice from financial professionals** - Financial professionals, such as financial planners and advisors, can provide valuable advice on financial matters.
4. **Use financial apps and tools** - There are many financial apps and tools available that can help you manage your finances and improve your financial literacy.
5. **Practice good financial habits** - Make a budget, save money, and invest wisely. By practicing good financial habits, you will improve your financial literacy over time.

Financial literacy is a vital skill in today's world. It enables individuals to make informed financial decisions, build wealth, and achieve financial independence. By improving your financial literacy, you can take control of your finances and build a secure financial future.

By Adriana Luna Carlos

HEALING FROM TRAUMA, GRIEF, AND LOSS

Writer : Clare Steffen, Ed.D.

For individuals who have experienced trauma or are experiencing grief or loss, the task of trying to block extraneous information due to hypervigilance or a tendency to hyper-focus may be even more difficult. The two behaviors of hyper-vigilance and hyper-focusing act like a switch in the brain that has been turned on and the off switch is broken. The constant stimulation and input of information can be overwhelming which leads to a heightened state of anxiety. Learning to identify triggers and ways to manage them is crucial. Many individuals turn to substances as a way to self-medicate in an effort to reduce the discomfort of anxiety.

Until recently, individuals with trauma had trouble receiving the right type of mental health treatment due to the complexity of their condition and the multiplicity of symptoms presented.

I have rewritten the 12 steps from AA to modernize the language and to specifically address issues related to trauma. They are shared here to introduce the reader to a different approach to recovery from trauma and substance use.

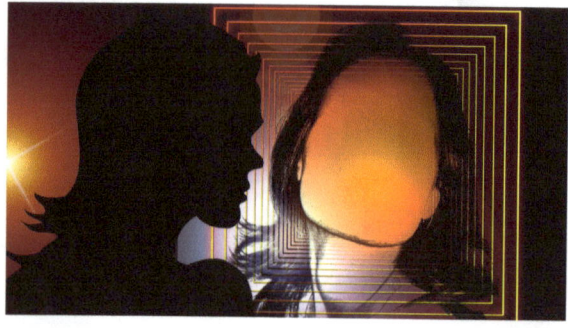

The Trauma Recovery Twelve Steps:

1. We recognize that the pleasure-reward system is triggered when we use substances and that we run the risk of life becoming unmanageable when we use.
2. Came to believe that restoring choice and building the skills needed to make healthy choices could restore our well-being.

3. Made a decision to connect with our true nature and find the courage to become our authentic selves.
4. Made an ongoing honest inventory of self in various environments and relationships.
5. Admitted to self and others our transgressions and plan to change and remedy our poor choices, errors in judgment, and harmful behaviors.
6. Made a commitment to develop character strengths and traits, and live a life of value, purpose, and meaning.
7. Admit our shortcomings and appreciate our gifts and attributes with humility.
8. Consider the people we have harmed and attempt to repair the relationship if possible, or if the other person so desires.
9. Learn to forgive self and others if possible, and when not, work on creating acceptance, forgiveness, or love.
10. Continue to personally assess the manner in which we live our lives and made a commitment to avoid the perpetration of trauma, chaos, or hurt.
11. Seek through prayer and meditation to heal and transcend our unhealthy past and to consciously determine an enlightened way of being.
12. Having had an opportunity to develop and restore wellness, we share these teachings with others to offer support and healing to an individual, families, and the community to promote recovery.

Twelve-Step to Trauma Recovery Inventory:

1. Ask yourself the benefits of using substances? In what way does this impact your ability to manage your life? What changes do you plan to make? How will you get there?

2. Examine your ability to make healthy choices. Do you know how to invite, investigate, and initiate choice? What changes do you plan to make? How will you get there?

3. What do you know about your authentic self? How do you connect to your true nature? What changes do you plan to make? How will you get there?

4. What do you love about yourself? In what environment or relationships do you connect to loving yourself? Are there changes you need to make to be healthy? What changes do you plan to make? How will you get there?

5. Are you able to take responsibility for your behaviors? How are you learning to make better choices? What healthy behaviors are you using to replace unhealthy behaviors? What changes do you plan to make? How will you maintain your new healthy behaviors?

6. Have you identified your character strengths and traits? Are you committed to living a life of value, purpose, and meaning? What changes do you need to make? How will you maintain them?

7. Do you know your shortcomings and can you apply your character strengths to balance them? Are you remaining humble? What changes do you need to make? How will you maintain them?

8. Have you taken inventory of any people you may have harmed and when possible, have you attempted to repair the relationship? What changes do you plan to make? How will you maintain them?

9. Have you forgiven yourself, and when possible, have you forgiven others? Are you working on acceptance, forgiveness, and love? What changes do you need to make? How will you maintain them?

10. Are you committed to living a healthy life? Are you actively avoiding the perpetuation of trauma, shame, chaos, or hurt in your life? What changes do you need to make? How will you maintain them?

11. How are you learning to rise above past hurts? Do you engage in mindful acts to become more enlightened? Do you have a healthy spiritual life? What changes do you need to make? How will you maintain them?

12. Are you engaged in giving back to others and are you part of a healing community? What change do you need to make? How will you maintain them?

Individuals who suffer from trauma oftentimes have disturbing and intrusive thoughts, images, perceptions, and flashbacks. Frequently, these occur without warning or because the individual has not yet identified their triggers or learned to manage them effectively. This causes them to experience dysregulation, which refers to emotional responses that are poorly regulated or do not display within a socially acceptable or expected range of emotional responses. They may be too intense or limited in the range of emotional responses.

Sleep disruption and nightmares or terrors are severe problems for many, and without good sleep hygiene people are at a higher risk for depression, anxiety, and a myriad of physical health risks and problems. Functioning under the condition of exhaustion is extremely difficult to manage. Managing stress effectively and making sure emotional support is readily available is crucial.

Reach out to Clare:
⊕ **claresteffen.com**
⊕ **brainiacbookstore.com**

UNLOCK YOUR TRUE POTENTIAL WITH DIONNE MALUSH: A JOURNEY OF GROWTH

In the world of real estate, success isn't just about transactions; it's about unlocking your true potential. Dionne Malush, co-owner of Realty ONE Group Gold Standard, is a visionary leader who embodies this ethos

Malush's background in graphic design has profoundly influenced her approach to real estate, particularly in marketing and branding strategies. At Realty ONE Group Gold Standard, she leverages her expertise to create visually captivating marketing materials that not only elevate agents but also strengthen the brokerage's brand presence in a competitive market. Her focus is on empowering agents to succeed, and her design prowess plays a crucial role in achieving this goal.

But Malush's journey doesn't stop there. As a leader of the Think and Grow Rich Mastermind, she imparts key insights from Napoleon Hill's principles to fuel personal and professional growth. These teachings, centered on positivity, goal-setting, and resilience, have shaped Malush's strategic thinking and decision-making processes, essential qualities for navigating the challenges of the real estate industry.

Driven by her passion for continual learning, Malush stays attuned to recent trends and developments in real estate, particularly the integration of technology. By incorporating innovations like AI into training programs, she equips agents with cutting-edge tools to stay ahead in the market and enhance their sales strategies.

Balancing roles as mentor, trainer, and co-owner, Malush devotes extensive time to training and development, ensuring agents are well-prepared to meet their goals.

Through regular training sessions and personal mentoring, she fosters a culture of continuous learning and innovation, ensuring the ongoing success of agents and the brokerage.

Realty ONE Group Gold Standard remains proactive in adapting to market dynamics, with a focus on teaching new strategies and scripts to equip agents for success.

By enhancing their online presence and integrating advanced technologies, the brokerage positions itself not just to adapt, but to lead in a dynamic industry.

Malush's passion for helping others unlock their full potential extends to her podcast, "Shine On Success," where she shares insights on overcoming adversity and achieving success. Launched in 2024, the podcast offers practical wisdom and inspiration, empowering listeners to shine in their endeavors.

As a certified B.A.N.K. IOS Trainer, Malush integrates personality-based sales strategies into recruitment processes, enhancing real estate practices and attracting new agents. By understanding client needs and communication styles, agents forge more effective interactions, giving the brokerage a unique competitive edge.

In the hands of Dionne Malush, real estate becomes more than just buying and selling; it becomes a journey of growth and empowerment. Are you ready to unlock your true potential? With Malush as your guide, the path to success is within reach.

CONNECT WITH DIONNE
WWW.LINKTR.EE/DIONNEMALUSH

WRITTEN BY
DIONNE MALUSH

WEBSITE
WWW.DIONNEMALUSH.COM/

Strong Beliefs - Empty Nester Moms

By Kim Damon

Waking up in the morning, I felt off. I mean, off! I'm just angry at the world, and I don't know why. Do you experience this? You get in the shower and start thinking about the day. Since you woke up on the wrong side of the bed, you start thinking about all the people who upset you, and you start to have imaginary arguments with them, which you usually win in your head. You have a full-blown argument in your head, and nothing has even happened yet.

Even as I backtrack and tell myself that nothing has gone wrong, I notice that I don't even want to be in the same room with myself. Then the anger turns inward. It's only about 10:00 am, and I still have the rest of the day to hang out with the angry me. It feels crazy like we don't know why we are mad, but we are mad about everything. I recognize this; It's Cognitive Dissonance. I feel it all the time with my adult children. There are many signs of Cognitive Dissonance, where our brain is arguing with itself. Today, my cognitive dissonance is that I'm upset but there is no reason to be upset.

It's that internal disagreement that takes place in our minds that makes us feel crazy or distressed without any clear reasoning. Parents of adults experience cognitive dissonance because we have beliefs or values that are running our brains. When moms of adults are suffering, the dissonance is crippling. "They don't care about me" – "Kids should respect their parents." "I'm embarrassed by my kid's behavior "- "They are good people and sometimes make bad choices." "I'm was a terrible mom" – "I did everything for them" "I want a glass of wine" – "Alcohol is not good for me" "My husband doesn't understand what I'm going through" – "He is a good man and supports me." When our thoughts, feelings, or actions do not match up with how we think we should think, act, or feel, the fight begins. And it feels like dipping our toes in craziness. How do we resolve this? First, realize that when this happens, you are human.

There are ways for us to keep the dissonance down when it feels strong. We can change our old beliefs if it's no longer helping us. We can change the way we behave now by changing our thoughts, feelings, and actions, or we can decide that our belief justifies no further engagement with the problem. I need to examine some of my beliefs. Yet, many of them are unwavering, and I'm good with that. They are my moral compass in life, and without some of them, I wouldn't know who I am as a woman, a partner, a mother, or a friend. Growing up, the only scuffles I had were protecting someone from being picked on. I even struggle with this as an adult. I fight the urge to jump right in and take sides, even to this day. I like this part of myself, but it also gets me in trouble. I once jumped into a rock fight with my cousins because it was two against one.

As I knelt to pick up a rock, the cousin that I was helping hit me square in the back of my head with a large piece of pavement. I still have a bald spot to remind me. We might think it's noble to have that strong belief, but is it? Just jumping into action and not pausing to understand the situation is not noble. It landed me a severe blow and several stitches. Here is what I find interesting about having a strong belief; we decide at a very young age what is right and what is wrong, what is good and what is bad. Many of our beliefs are developed by the time we are 6 or 7 years old. Now, I don't know about you, but I don't trust my six-year-old self to decide what to believe. When we examine our beliefs, we get to decide if they are helping us or causing us to suffer more. When they are no longer helpful, we can change them. Letting go of outdated beliefs and clarifying our core values prevents most cognitive dissonance. Writing them down and identifying their origins allows us to discard what no longer serves and refine what does. By cleaning them up with better definitions and kinder words, we offer others the grace to believe differently. This process opens better lines of communication and reduces suffering, especially for moms of adults. Staying true to our core values empowers us, and we alone have the power to choose which ones to uphold.

www.midlifediscoveries.com | www.facebook.com/midlifediscoveries | www.instagram.com/midlifediscycrieskd

Emotional Health Effects Mental Health And Is Compounded With Each Generation!

Written By Shae Regan

As a Positive Mindset Mentor; Positive Parenting Consultant; Relationship Guide; and creator of Health Burst, a simple, effective, natural methodology designed to restore health, and free the mindset and body of " Inflammation Pollution," so one can lose weight and find their body again functions as nature intended;

I've seen a decline in several corresponding areas that seem to be overlooked as contributors to mental health.

Mental Health Issues appear to be more prominent presently than in the last century.
Equally more prominent is the amount of people in general, who become unprepared parents, failing at teaching their children about life 1.01, accountability, responsibility, and that one must apply one's self to reap beneficial fruits of successful ideas starting with: conception, planning, choices, follow- through, adaptability, and completion!

Too many parents have become parents without the ability to provide the emotional support a child needs. They often cannot even provide the basics to their children: food, shelter, clothing, safety, and guidance. They struggle trying to "do it all" for lack of preparation. They are preoccupied with working due to one-parent households. They can't teach what they don't know and haven't lived by example!

Essential elements are then missing for a child's balanced, encouraging mental and emotional growth, as well as their physical needs for healthy development.

Each generation suffers more than the last with stress and anxiety that would be unnecessary if planning took precedence over emotional satiation!

When parents are stressed, children know, and subsequently, they absorb and harbor that stress, because they have little control to effect change. That lingers and affects people into adulthood because such circumstances are the child's "normal."

Often, when the children reach adulthood, they struggle with wanting to avoid, and yet magnetically gravitating to the same because it's what they "know"!

If parents argue, children will find mates to recreate a similar scenario. If parents struggle with finances, the child often has an attraction/fear relationship to money. If parents don't address challenges, the child often can be "avoidant."

Then add to that the "food-like substances" often purchased on a tight budget do not offer nutritious sustenance for growing minds and bodies. They don't support adult bodies' needs either.

This further stresses out the body, like starving it. Lack of nutrients leads to lack of energy, which leads to lack of circulation, which leads to lack of brain health, and so on.

Additionally, people often turn to medications for headaches, aches and pains and other issues, which further fractures the body's natural functions to deal with stress and healing; instead of turning to simple natural answers: eating well, hydration, sleeping enough working at something one enjoys and is talented at doing!

The "breakdown" can be profound, and compounds with each generation. With that, often comes anger, less emotional control, wanting more, and having less opportunities because the mind doesn't perform well under stress. Cognition diminishes. Comprehension is difficult. Retention is challenging. Those all add more to the original stresses!

A mind in a deeply stressful situation is in "survival mode." It's mild to severe PTSD!

It's difficult to predict what someone can do in "survival mode." Anything is possible, from lifting a car off of someone to manipulation to arguing constantly, to stealing, to physical fights, to harming people!

The drop in mental health and the increases in outbursts, of emotional unwellness, bullying, and violence, all coincide with the lack of teaching how to care for one's self, and love and serve in the capacity of one's passion and purpose.

Productive, positively energized people, focus on honing and sharing their abilities, helping others to improve their lives and create success.

Productive, positive people are busy planning their next steps to connect to more people, to share more of their journey, their triumphs, their challenges, and the fruits of all the learning processes with more people!

How do people become positively charged and productive?

Instead of looking to others to do for them, tell them what to do, when, and for how long; productive, purposed people look both inwardly and up!

Too many people have lost sight of the bigger picture that we are all a part of the journey together.

We are all created for a purpose, that only we can achieve. No matter what your beliefs may be, we are here to complete a mission to love and serve. One's likes, gifts, talents, and passions, are the hints to follow, to hone, to experience, and to gain confidence and presence. Then we must share and affect someone's life for the better!

People will become attracted to the altruistic care offered and a business can emerge.
"If you love what you do, you never work a day in your life." You live what you love!

Simple ways to achieve mental, emotional, spiritual, and physical health are:

- Take time to care for yourself.
- Eat healthy whole foods.
- Sleep eight hours.
- Walk for 30 minutes at leisure and look up in awe that you are alive, here and now!
- Write down, pray, or say grace before eating, sleeping, taking action, and making a decision about what you are thankful, grateful, and appreciative of in your life!
- Remain teachable, open, and receptive.
- Be ready, willing, and available to share what you know, when needed and appropriate, and to know when that is.
- Be respectful of yourself and others!
- If you offend, immediately tend to "the broken slat on the bridge" to avoid more damage or burning that bridge!
- create resources from connections and synergy. Working with others creates more options and opportunities!
- Make your bed every day! Even if everything tanks that day, at least you accomplished one thing! And you can go to sleep in a comfy, neat bed!

I've seen amazing paradigm shifts in people's lives from this simple approach! Remember, "like forces" are attracted, so choose to be positive and "see" your decisions leading to success in your Mindset. Your mind will always prove you're right.

Those mindset methods combat mental illness in ways you can direct!

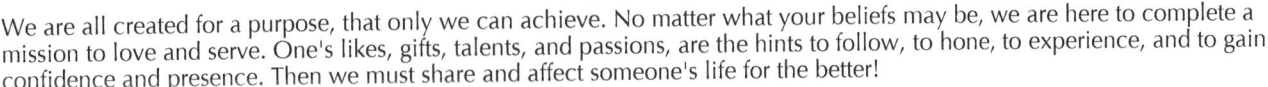

www.facebook.com/ShaeRegan | www.instagram.com/ShaeRegan HealthBurst

CREATING SPACE - MENTAL ILLNESS

CRISTINA CALERO

Where do you take cover when you don't have shelter? Where do you find safety when all seems threatening? In whose arms do you find comfort when they are holding someone else?

It started with a light, gentle rain. Barely audible within the cozy walls of a quaint little cottage by the sea, but pounded like hailstones on the tarp of my new home. 'Home'... that word would soon become heat in everyone's mouth as it fired the topic of conversation and morphed into a primal need that would break the mind and the spirit of so many. As the gentle rain turned to an apocalyptic flood; a tsunami of grief gripped our land as the unbridled power of Mother Nature was unleashed, again, and again. She was creating space at an unbelievable cost.

I was one of the lucky ones. I had a roof over my head. My new home was a caravan in the driveway of my sister and brother-in-law's rental. Cruisy Van Go was damp, moldy, cramped, an oven under the Sun, an icebox under the Moon, and I loved it! Cruisy and I didn't float away, didn't catch on fire, didn't get ransacked by looters, didn't fall apart under the weight of water that seemed to attack from all angles, and didn't lose power. But we did cry and joined in the collective head-shaking question 'How will people come back from this?!' A couple of years on and that question is showing up as amazing stories of resilience, determination, and a sheer will to survive, with or without a 'home'.

My mum used to ask me "Why aren't you making music my darling?" and my answer was nearly always along the lines of "Because I am just trying to stay alive".

When post-traumatic stress takes hold and manifests as a myriad of dysfunctions that range from the annoying to completely debilitating; the adage of 'just trying to get through the day' rings in our ears. My ears had been ringing for a number of years prior to stepping over the narrow threshold of the little caravan, but I knew I had found a 'space to create'. I felt 'safe'. To climb out of that deep well of trauma required a rope and now that I had a home, now that I had – 'survived', I was determined to find that friggen rope.

I had my laptop, I had clothes, I had coffee, and I had insomnia. And now, I also had time.

The rope came.

Wiping tears from your eyes can make for slippery hands and so, gripping that rope was not an easy endeavour. It slipped, it whipped, it tore through my strength but I just had to get my head above that wave and try living again. Grief can wake you, but so too can a creative project, and in those silent hours often a voice can be heard that asks 'Which one will you give your energy to... now that you're awake?'. To keep going, you have to find the tools to keep going. Mental illness has its habits, its patterns, and its preferred modes of operandi, and it can be a case of trial and error; finding the tools that circumvent those modes and take you to the edge of a shore that you thought you may never set foot on again.

Creating space left me with few options; the most comfortable being – standing next to the kitchen sink, laptop propped on a tupperware container, van window open in daylight hours to let light, air, and smiles in, and closed at night to keep the mozzies out. Hours of standing and pouring my focus into creating had afforded me relief from downward spirals of negativity. Having an anchor for my days gave me gentle ripples of growing self-esteem, for which peeing in a pot had been the final act of erosion. I created a document with an outline of 1. Tasks to finish today 2. Goals for the week 3. Ideas for Project A 4. Ideas for Project B 5. People to call asap 6. People to call one month before completion etc. I then created a document for each of the numbered topics and pretty coloured folders to house the finished items. AMAZING! The power of FOCUSED distraction, an oxymoron that became the muse for my creations; can be quite gentle in leading us out of mental illness. It leaves scope for interpretation and for alteration, for those days when rolling over to face the wall is all that can be managed. Focused distraction under the wing of creation, allowed me to have compassion for what I was trying to accomplish - creating space; space in my mind, space in my heart, space in my biases, space in my outpouring of sadness, space in my calendar, space in my days, space from the past. There is so much power in being gentle and allowing space.

Since 2020 the escalation in mental illness is unfathomable. And yet, in the wake of so much suffering, so much grief, so much displacement, there has been an explosion of creativity. We are programmed to CREATE! Entelechy is our NATURE! Our unrealised potential is so much at the core of why we continue to suffer beyond the initial wound and it's worth every effort we can muster, to find a way to express that potential.

The stunning examples of how others have found their way through this suffering are beautifully illustrated in the powerful painting of artist Karla Dickens by Indigenous artist Black Douglas. The 2022 winner of the prestigious Archibald Prize shows Karla wading through flood water carrying buckets filled to the brim with muddy invaders, and eyes filled to the brim with determination.

We can create a Heaven of this Hell.

🌐 focusmindplusbody.com
📷 @focusmindplusbody
📷 @calerocstars

THE SHE RISES STUDIOS PODCAST

The She Rises Studios podcast is dedicated to empowering women like you to reach their full potential and live their best lives. With inspiring stories, insightful interviews, and practical advice from experts in different industries, our podcast is your go-to source for information, inspiration, and motivation. Join us as we explore topics like:

- Overcoming self-doubt and limiting beliefs
- Building and running a successful business
- Building confidence and Self-esteem
- Navigating career transitions
- Starting and growing a business
- Balancing work and family life
- Improving physical and mental health
- Finding meaning and purpose in life
- So many more

Our guests include successful entrepreneurs, inspiring thought leaders, and everyday women who have overcome challenges and achieved their dreams. Each episode is packed with actionable tips and strategies to help you take your life to the next level.

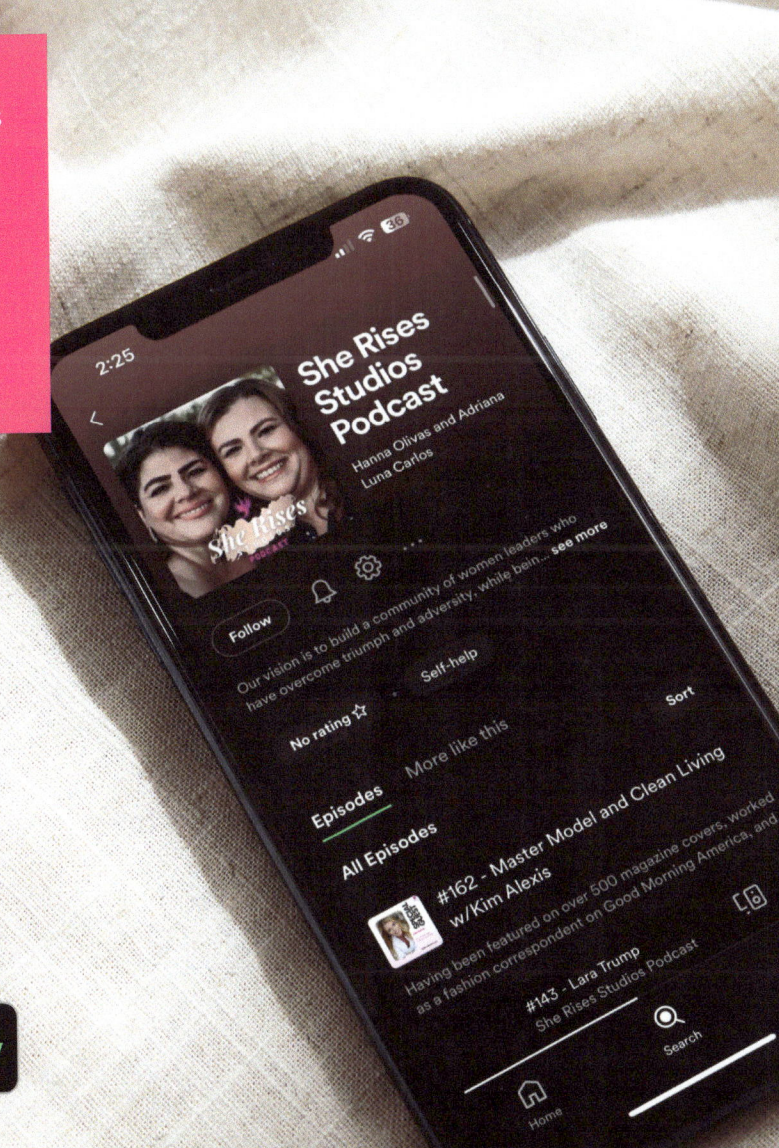

www.ingramcontent.com/pod-product-compliance
Lightning Source LLC
Chambersburg PA
CBHW041435120626
46547CB00002B/234